Vocabulary Tales™

Kitty Breaks the Bank

by Pamela Chanko
illustrated by Jannie Ho

SCHOLASTIC INC.
New York • Toronto • London • Auckland • Sydney
Mexico City • New Delhi • Hong Kong • Buenos Aires

Designed by Maria Lilja
ISBN-13: 978-0-545-08875-6 • ISBN-10: 0-545-08875-5

First printing, January 2009
12 11 10 9 8 7 6 5 4 3 2 1 9 10 11 12 13 14/0

Building Vocabulary With This Book

This book contains eight key words that are important for all children to know. Read the story straight through for enjoyment. Then read it again, pausing to define and discuss each key word. Follow-up the tale with the fun activities on pages 14–16. When you're done, celebrate—kids will have added eight great words to their vocabularies!

Kitty woke up on a day that was sunny.
"I'll go shopping!" she said.
"I'll spend some of my money."

KEY WORD: **allowance**

Simple Definition: money that is given to someone regularly

Sample Sentence: My mom gives me an *allowance* of five dollars a week.

She had saved her **allowance** and locked it away. Now she would spend it! Today was the day!

KEY WORD: dollar

Simple Definition: the main unit of money; one *dollar* is equal to 100 cents

Sample Sentence: I couldn't buy a computer game because I only had five *dollars* in my pocket.

Kitty packed up her purse. She was all set.
She had thirty-two **dollars**. What should she get?

KEY WORD: **quarter**

Simple Definition: a coin that is equal to 25 cents

Sample Sentence: You can put a *quarter* into the gumball machine to get a gumball.

The gumdrops looked yummy, yet candy goes fast.
They were only a **quarter**, but gumdrops don't last.

KEY WORD: **price**

Simple Definition: the amount that you have to pay for something

Sample Sentence: The *price* of that teddy bear is twenty dollars.

She saw a nice dress, and the **price** was just right.
But the dress didn't fit. No, the dress was too tight.

KEY WORD: cent

Simple Definition: the smallest unit of money; the value of a penny

Sample Sentence: At the penny-candy store, you can buy lots of candy for only a few *cents*.

She could buy pretty curtains for ninety-nine **cents**.
But the colors were wrong, so that didn't make sense.

She found a warm coat, soft and furry to touch.

KEY WORD: **bargain**

Simple Definition: something that you buy for less than the usual price

Sample Sentence: The shirt was a *bargain* because it was on sale for half price.

But it wasn't a **bargain**. It cost way too much!

KEY WORD: **dime**

Simple Definition: a coin that is equal to ten cents

Sample Sentence: If you have ten pennies in your pocket, you can trade them for a *dime*.

She looked and she looked for a very long time. But nothing was right. She had not spent a **dime**!

At the end of the day, she had tried every store.
There was nothing she needed. Why shop anymore?

At home, Mama Cat asked, "What did you buy?"
"Nothing!" said Kitty. And she started to cry.

KEY WORD: **free**

Simple Definition: not costing any money

Sample Sentence: If you can't decide what ice-cream flavor you want, most shops will give you a *free* taste.

"What you need is a hug," Mama said. "Come to me." Mama was right—and guess what? It was **free**!

Meaning Match

money words

Listen to the definition. Then go to the WORD CHEST and find a vocabulary word that matches it.

1. the amount that you have to pay for something
2. a coin that is equal to ten cents
3. the main unit of money; one is equal to 100 cents
4. something that you buy for less than the usual price
5. a coin that is equal to 25 cents
6. the smallest unit of money; the value of a penny
7. not costing any money
8. money that is given to someone regularly

Answers: 1. price 2. dime 3. dollar 4. bargain 5. quarter 6. cent 7. free 8. allowance

Vocabulary Fill-ins

money words

Listen to the sentence. Then go to the WORD BOX and find the best word to fill in the blank.

WORD BOX

free	dollar	quarter	price
cent	allowance	dime	bargain

1. The __________ of that board game is 18 dollars.

2. The grocery store was giving away _______ samples of cheese.
3. When I turn seven, my parents are going to start giving me an _________.
4. One penny is equal to one _________.
5. A _________ is equal to 25 cents.
6. Tim used four quarters to buy a magazine that cost one _________.
7. Molly had a _________ so she bought a ten-cent piece of bubblegum.
8. I got this coat on sale for half price. What a _________!

Answers: 1. price 2. free 3. allowance 4. cent 5. quarter 6. dollar 7. dime 8. bargain

Vocabulary Questions

money words

Listen to each question. Think about it. Then answer.

1. Would you rather have one **dollar** or 10 nickels? Tell why.
2. What is something you enjoy that is **free**? Why do you like it?
3. Would you rather have one **quarter** or 25 pennies? Why?
4. Do you think kids should have to do chores in order to get an **allowance**? Why or why not?
5. What **price** would you pay to get one wish to come true? What would your wish be, and why would this be a fair **price**?
6. If someone gave you a penny, which is worth one **cent**, what would you do with it?
7. A **dime** is smaller than a penny or a nickel. Does that mean it's worth less?
8. Did you ever go shopping and get a **bargain**? Tell about it.

Extra: Can you think of some more money words? Make a list.